This book belongs to:

Password Safety Tips:

Make your passwords long

Make them a nonsense phrase

Include numbers and symbols

Avoid using personal info

Do not reuse passwords

Use a password manager app

Don't give them to anyone else

Change passwords regularly

Internet Address / URL:

Website Name:

Username:

Password:

Notes:

Internet Address / URL:

Website Name:

Username:

Password:

Notes:

0-9

Internet Address / URL:

Website Name:

Username:

Password:

Notes:

Internet Address / URL:

Website Name:

Username:

Password:

Notes:

Internet Address / URL:

Website Name:

Username:

Password:

Notes:

Internet Address / URL:

Website Name:

Username:

Password:

Notes:

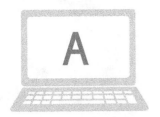

Internet Address / URL:

Website Name:

Username:

Password:

Notes:

Internet Address / URL:

Website Name:

Username:

Password:

Notes:

B

Internet Address / URL:

Website Name:

Username:

Password:

Notes:

Internet Address / URL:

Website Name:

Username:

Password:

Notes:

Internet Address / URL:

Website Name:

Username:

Password:

Notes:

Internet Address / URL:

Website Name:

Username:

Password:

Notes:

Internet Address / URL:

Website Name:

Username:

Password:

Notes:

Internet Address / URL:

Website Name:

Username:

Password:

Notes:

Internet Address / URL:

Website Name:

Username:

Password:

Notes:

Internet Address / URL:

Website Name:

Username:

Password:

Notes:

Internet Address / URL:

Website Name:

Username:

Password:

Notes:

Internet Address / URL:

Website Name:

Username:

Password:

Notes:

Internet Address / URL:

Website Name:

Username:

Password:

Notes:

Internet Address / URL:

Website Name:

Username:

Password:

Notes:

Internet Address / URL:

Website Name:

Username:

Password:

Notes:

Internet Address / URL:

Website Name:

Username:

Password:

Notes:

Internet Address / URL:

Website Name:

Username:

Password:

Notes:

Internet Address / URL:

Website Name:

Username:

Password:

Notes:

Internet Address / URL:

Website Name:

Username:

Password:

Notes:

Internet Address / URL:

Website Name:

Username:

Password:

Notes:

Internet Address / URL:

Website Name:

Username:

Password:

Notes:

Internet Address / URL:

Website Name:

Username:

Password:

Notes:

Internet Address / URL:

Website Name:

Username:

Password:

Notes:

Internet Address / URL:

Website Name:

Username:

Password:

Notes:

Internet Address / URL:

Website Name:

Username:

Password:

Notes:

Internet Address / URL:

Website Name:

Username:

Password:

Notes:

Internet Address / URL:

Website Name:

Username:

Password:

Notes:

Internet Address / URL:

Website Name:

Username:

Password:

Notes:

Internet Address / URL:

Website Name:

Username:

Password:

Notes:

Internet Address / URL:

Website Name:

Username:

Password:

Notes:

Internet Address / URL:

Website Name:

Username:

Password:

Notes:

Internet Address / URL:

Website Name:

Username:

Password:

Notes:

Internet Address / URL:

Website Name:

Username:

Password:

Notes:

Internet Address / URL:

Website Name:

Username:

Password:

Notes:

Internet Address / URL:

Website Name:

Username:

Password:

Notes:

Internet Address / URL:

Website Name:

Username:

Password:

Notes:

Internet Address / URL:

Website Name:

Username:

Password:

Notes:

Internet Address / URL:

Website Name:

Username:

Password:

Notes:

Internet Address / URL:

Website Name:

Username:

Password:

Notes:

Internet Address / URL:

Website Name:

Username:

Password:

Notes:

Internet Address / URL:

Website Name:

Username:

Password:

Notes:

Internet Address / URL:

Website Name:

Username:

Password:

Notes:

Internet Address / URL:

Website Name:

Username:

Password:

Notes:

Internet Address / URL:

Website Name:

Username:

Password:

Notes:

Internet Address / URL:

Website Name:

Username:

Password:

Notes:

Internet Address / URL:

Website Name:

Username:

Password:

Notes:

Internet Address / URL:

Website Name:

Username:

Password:

Notes:

Internet Address / URL:

Website Name:

Username:

Password:

Notes:

Internet Address / URL:

Website Name:

Username:

Password:

Notes:

Internet Address / URL:

Website Name:

Username:

Password:

Notes:

Internet Address / URL:

Website Name:

Username:

Password:

Notes:

Internet Address / URL:

Website Name:

Username:

Password:

Notes:

Internet Address / URL:

Website Name:

Username:

Password:

Notes:

Internet Address / URL:

Website Name:

Username:

Password:

Notes:

Internet Address / URL:

Website Name:

Username:

Password:

Notes:

Internet Address / URL:

Website Name:

Username:

Password:

Notes:

Internet Address / URL:

Website Name:

Username:

Password:

Notes:

Internet Address / URL:

Website Name:

Username:

Password:

Notes:

Internet Address / URL:

Website Name:

Username:

Password:

Notes:

Internet Address / URL:

Website Name:

Username:

Password:

Notes:

Internet Address / URL:

Website Name:

Username:

Password:

Notes:

Internet Address / URL:

Website Name:

Username:

Password:

Notes:

Internet Address / URL:

Website Name:

Username:

Password:

Notes:

Internet Address / URL:

Website Name:

Username:

Password:

Notes:

Internet Address / URL:

Website Name:

Username:

Password:

Notes:

Internet Address / URL:

Website Name:

Username:

Password:

Notes:

Internet Address / URL:

Website Name:

Username:

Password:

Notes:

Internet Address / URL:

Website Name:

Username:

Password:

Notes:

Internet Address / URL:

Website Name:

Username: Password:

Notes:

Internet Address / URL:

Website Name:

Username:

Password:

Notes:

Internet Address / URL:

Website Name:

Username:

Password:

Notes:

Internet Address / URL:

Website Name:

Username:

Password:

Notes:

Internet Address / URL:

Website Name:

Username: Password:

Notes:

Internet Address / URL:

Website Name:

Username:

Password:

Notes:

Internet Address / URL:

Website Name:

Username:

Password:

Notes:

Internet Address / URL:

Website Name:

Username:

Password:

Notes:

Internet Address / URL:

Website Name:

Username:

Password:

Notes:

Internet Address / URL:

Website Name:

Username:

Password:

Notes:

Internet Address / URL:

Website Name:

Username:

Password:

Notes:

Internet Address / URL:

Website Name:

Username:

Password:

Notes:

Internet Address / URL:

Website Name:

Username:

Password:

Notes:

Internet Address / URL:

Website Name:

Username:

Password:

Notes:

Internet Address / URL:

Website Name:

Username:

Password:

Notes:

Internet Address / URL:

Website Name:

Username:

Password:

Notes:

Internet Address / URL:

Website Name:

Username:

Password:

Notes:

Internet Address / URL:

Website Name:

Username:

Password:

Notes:

Internet Address / URL:

Website Name:

Username:

Password:

Notes:

Internet Address / URL:

Website Name:

Username:

Password:

Notes:

Internet Address / URL:

Website Name:

Username:

Password:

Notes:

Internet Address / URL:

Website Name:

Username:

Password:

Notes:

Internet Address / URL:

Website Name:

Username:

Password:

Notes:

Internet Address / URL:

Website Name:

Username:

Password:

Notes:

Internet Address / URL:

Website Name:

Username:

Password:

Notes:

Internet Address / URL:

Website Name:

Username:

Password:

Notes:

Internet Address / URL:

Website Name:

Username:

Password:

Notes:

Internet Address / URL:

Website Name:

Username:

Password:

Notes:

Internet Address / URL:

Website Name:

Username:

Password:

Notes:

Internet Address / URL:

Website Name:

Username:

Password:

Notes:

Internet Address / URL:

Website Name:

Username:

Password:

Notes:

Internet Address / URL:

Website Name:

Username:

Password:

Notes:

Internet Address / URL:

Website Name:

Username:

Password:

Notes:

Internet Address / URL:

Website Name:

Username:

Password:

Notes:

Notes:

Notes:

Notes:

Notes:

Notes:

Notes:

Notes:

Notes:

Notes:

Notes:

www.ingramcontent.com/pod-product-compliance
Lightning Source LLC
Chambersburg PA
CBHW052147070326
40689CB00050B/2439